Mystics
a guide to happiness

Mystics
a guide to happiness

WRITTEN AND COMPILED BY **TERESA DE BERTODANO**

A LION BOOK

Copyright © 2003 Teresa de Bertodano
This edition copyright © 2003
Lion Publishing

The author asserts the moral right to
be identified as the author of this work

Published by
Lion Publishing plc
Mayfield House, 256 Banbury Road,
Oxford OX2 7DH, England
www.lion-publishing.co.uk
ISBN 0 7459 5098 1

First edition 2003
10 9 8 7 6 5 4 3 2 1 0

A catalogue record for this book is
available from the British Library

Typeset in 9.5/15 GillSans Light
Printed in Singapore

Contents

Introduction

It isn't hard to be a mystic. All we have
to do is fall in love with God; the rest
will follow.

CATHERINE DE HUECK DOHERTY (1896–1985)

When we want to know more
about a particular sport or skill,
we are likely to watch or read
about the top performers. Such
people have much to teach us –
but it is obvious that they are not
the only practitioners. Apart from
the many amateurs, there may also
be individuals who equal the top
players, but who have chosen to
stay out of the limelight. The world
will never know of their existence.

In the area of Christian
mysticism, we usually hear about
the major players – St Augustine
of Hippo, St Teresa of Avila, Thomas
Merton or Anthony de Mello – and,
of course, the greatest mystic of all:
Jesus himself. But the big names are
not the only ones. There are many
others whose names echo down
the centuries. It is impossible to
know the total number of mystics,
but the figure may run into millions.
Towards the end of her short life,
St Thérèse of Lisieux remarked,
'Perhaps I owe all the graces with
which I am laden to some soul
whom I shall only know in heaven.'

The Oxford Dictionary
describes a mystic as one
who 'believes in the spiritual
apprehension of truths that are
beyond the understanding'. At the
start of the twenty-first century, it
seems possible that the number of
mystics is increasing. Some may not
be living in conventionally religious
situations; others may be in prison
or in psychiatric hospitals. Many
would not dream of describing

themselves as 'mystics', and may not even be familiar with the word.

If that great thirteenth-century mystic St Francis of Assisi had been alive today, the 'extreme' manifestations of his love for God and for creation might well have earned him a place in a psychiatric ward. The Francis who allowed his tunic to catch light and then refused to douse the flames for fear of harming 'brother fire' would very probably find himself diagnosed as a danger to himself and to others. Fortunately for Francis, his brethren did not share his concern for 'brother fire' and were quick to extinguish the flames! Most mystics are less extreme than Francis, but anyone who has fallen deeply in love with God may act and express themselves in ways that seem crazy to the rest of the world.

The language and actions of those who have fallen in love for the first time (or even for the fifth or sixth time) may seem inexplicable and repetitive to family and friends. When the lovers cannot be together, they may insist on talking about the object of their affections to the exclusion of all else! It can be the same with the mystics. If they are not with God in prayer, then they are talking about him and pouring out their love to anybody who will listen.

In *Mystics: A Guide to Happiness,*

we meet some big names, including St Francis de Sales and St Thérèse of Lisieux, St John of the Cross and Mother Teresa of Calcutta. But this book also contains insights from others who may be less widely known outside their own country: Australia's Mary MacKillop, America's Cardinal Joseph Bernardin and England's Ronald Knox. In the words of the late Cardinal Basil Hume of Westminster, 'The thread that binds [the mystics] is a passionate love of God and a willingness to be still, to "waste time with God" (often in the midst of hectic lives) and to allow God to love them.'

TERESA DE BERTODANO
2 JANUARY 2003

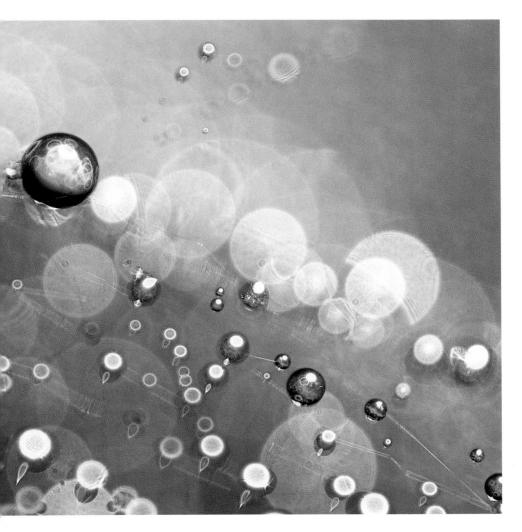

The Love of God

Many of us wonder whether there really is any sort of a God to believe in – let alone to love. Life sometimes seems to be falling apart, and if there is a God 'up there', why doesn't he come down here and do something about the atrocities in the world, not to mention my own problems? The mystics were very familiar with the difficulty of believing in God at all – let alone believing in a loving God. Their most sublime outpourings of love were sometimes written in blind faith and mental wretchedness. They were determined to believe that there really was a God and that he loved them – and that he loves humanity. Were the mystics suffering from delusions? We may think so, but the evidence of their contemporaries indicates that the mystics possessed an inner peace and happiness when the exterior circumstances of their lives could have led them into despair. In their writings, we meet a God who loves each individual more than we can begin to imagine, a God who not only loves us, but who enters deeply into our sufferings and joys.

What no eye has seen, nor ear heard,
    nor the human heart conceived,
what God has prepared for
    those who love him.

1 CORINTHIANS 2:9

Blessed be the child who today
    delights Bethlehem.
Blessed be the newborn who today
    made humanity young again.
Blessed be the fruit who bowed
    himself down for our hunger.

Blessed be the gracious one who
      suddenly enriched all of our
      poverty and filled our need.

ST EPHREM THE SYRIAN (c. 306–73)

Cast yourself on him and do
not be afraid: he will not step
back and let you fall. Cast yourself
upon him trustfully; he will support
and heal you.

ST AUGUSTINE OF HIPPO (354–430)

In your prayers there is no need
for high-flown words, for it is
the simple and unsophisticated
babblings of children that have
more often won the heart of the
Father in heaven.

ST JOHN CLIMACUS (c. 570–c. 649)

Drawn by your fragrance
      the Bee flies down to you
from the splendour of the Father,
your calyx closes round him
      and shuts him in.

ST HILDEGARD OF BINGEN (1098–1179)

My soul cannot bear the agony
to chase the sinner away from me.

ST MECHTILD OF MAGDEBURG (c. 1207–c. 1282)

If the lover's love is not sufficient to
move his Beloved to pity and forgiveness, the Beloved's love is sufficient to
give grace and blessings to his creatures.

RAMON LULL (c. 1233–c. 1315)

He is our living paradise, for within
him and from out of him flows the
spring of eternal health, while from
his wounds flows balm, a medicine
which cures every sickness.

BLESSED JAN VAN RUUSBROEC (1293–1381)

O immeasurably tender love! Who
would not be set afire with such love?
What heart could keep from breaking?
You, deep well of charity, it seems
you are so madly in love with your
creatures that you could not live
without us! Yet you are our God,
and have no need of us.

ST CATHERINE OF SIENA (c. 1347–80)

You are the well that is always full and
always overflowing, the fire that burns
continually, never dying down.

ST THOMAS À KEMPIS (c. 1380–1471)

Christ when he died
deceived the cross:
and on death's side
threw all the loss,
the captive world awaked and found
the prisoner loose, the jailor bound.

RICHARD CRASHAW (c. 1613–49)

All which I took from thee
        I did but take,
    not for thy harms,
but just that thou might'st
        seek it in My arms.
    All which thy child's mistake
fancies as lost, I have stored
        for thee at home:
    rise, clasp My hand, and come!

FRANCIS THOMPSON (1859–1907)

O my three, my all, my beatitude,
infinite solitude, immensity in which

I lose myself, I yield myself to you as
a prey. Bury yourself in me that I may
bury myself in you, until I depart to
contemplate in your light the abyss
of your splendours.

BLESSED ELIZABETH OF THE TRINITY

(1880–1906)

The words *compelle intrare*, compel
them to come in, have been so abused
by wicked men that we shudder at
them; but, properly understood, they
plumb the depth of the divine mercy.
The hardness of God is kinder than the
softness of men, and his compulsion is
our liberation.

C.S. LEWIS (1893–1963)

No law court could function on the
principle of the parable of the prodigal
son, nor business flourish on that of
the labourers in the vineyard. But
God's ways are not our ways and
in his dealings with us justice is
swallowed up by mercy.

ROBERT LLEWELYN (1909–)

Do not worry about what you ought
to do. Worry about loving. Do not
interrogate heaven repeatedly and
uselessly, saying, 'What course of action
should I pursue?' Concentrate on
loving instead.

CARLO CARRETTO (1910–88)

Hate the obscuring sin, but not the soul,
the soul you made
    and you alone can see,
the golden secret hidden in the scroll.

DIANA MOMBER (1919–)

Once, while preaching in a parish,
I suddenly caught sight of a young
mother with her child and you
could see the love between them.
I was terribly tempted to say to the
congregation: 'Forget what I am saying
and look over there, and you will see
what we mean to God!'

CARDINAL BASIL HUME (1923–99)

The King of Love must be enthroned
in our mind and heart, take undivided

possession of our will and make of our very bodies the temples of the Holy Ghost.

METROPOLITAN ANTHONY OF SOUROZH (1914–)

We must go to this child, this man, the Son of God, at whatever inconvenience, at whatever risk to ourselves, because to know and love him will truly change our lives.

POPE JOHN PAUL II (1920–)

We only exist because God chooses to continue singing us into being.

IAN PETIT (1922–96)

Am I not the Almighty God? But if I choose to be loved, here and now, by your limited heart in preference to more perfect love… will you refuse…? Can you refuse…?

SOURCE UNTRACED

Prayer

The Oxford Dictionary describes prayer as 'a solemn request or thanksgiving to God or an object of worship' – which doesn't sound like any sort of a conversation with the God who is longing for us to share our worries and concerns with him, and to meet him exactly as we are and where we are. Perhaps we have been brought up to believe that God is a sort of auxiliary policeman – always watching us in order to catch us out in wrongdoing. Many of us have rightly stopped believing in such a God. The God whom Jesus and the mystics reveal to us is certainly watching us all the time – but only because he loves us so much that he cannot take his eyes off us.

When you pray, go into a room
by yourself, shut the door, and pray
to your Father who is in secret; and
your Father who sees what is done
in secret will reward you.

MATTHEW 6:6

Ah, Lord, love me passionately, love
me often, love me long. For the more
continuously you love me, the purer I
will be; the more fervently you love
me, the more beautiful I will be; the
longer you love me, the holier I will
become here on earth.

ST MECHTILD OF MAGDEBURG (c. 1207–c. 1282)

You who want knowledge
    seek the oneness within.
There you will find
    the clear mirror already waiting.

HADEWIJCH OF BRABANT (13TH CENTURY)

Each recognition of truth through
grace, felt with inward savour and
spiritual delight, is a secret whisper
from Jesus in the ear of a pure soul.

WALTER HILTON (c. 1343–96)

Set yourself to rest in this darkness
as long as you can, always crying
out after him whom you love.
For if you are to experience him
or to see him at all, insofar as it is
possible here, it must always be in
this cloud.

THE CLOUD OF UNKNOWING **(14TH CENTURY)**

So dark the night! At rest
and hushed my house, I went
    with no one knowing
upon a lover's quest
– Ah, the sheer grace! – so blest,
my eager heart with love
    aflame and glowing.

In darkness, hid from sight
I went by secret ladder safe and sure
– Ah, grace of sheer delight! –
so softly veiled by night,
hushed now my house,
    in darkness and secure.

ST JOHN OF THE CROSS (1542–91)

Offer him your heart from time to
time in the course of the day, amid
your labours, at any time you can. Do
not fetter yourself by rules or special
forms of worship. Act in faith, with
love, and with humility.

BROTHER LAWRENCE (c. 1614–91)

I felt my heart strangely warmed. I felt
I did trust in Christ, Christ alone, for
salvation: and an assurance was given
me, that he had taken away my sins,
even mine, and saved me from the
law of sin and death.

JOHN WESLEY (1703–91)

Earth's crammed with heaven,
and every common bush
    afire with God;
but only he who sees,
    takes off his shoes,
the rest sit round it
    and pluck blackberries,
and daub their natural faces unaware.

ELIZABETH BARRETT BROWNING (1806–61)

Take my love; my Lord I pour
at thy feet its treasure-store;
take myself, and I will be
ever, only all for thee.

CATHERINE BOOTH (1829–90)

To lift up the hands in prayer gives
God glory, but a man with a dungfork
in his hand, a woman with a slop-pail,
give him glory too. He is so great that

all things give him glory if you mean
they should.

GERARD MANLEY HOPKINS (1844–89)

The rule is simply: 'Pray as you can,
and do not try to pray as you can't.'
Take yourself as you find yourself,
and start from that.

ABBOT JOHN CHAPMAN (1865–1933)

If you feel drawn 'to rest in God',
to let yourself sink down as it were
into him, do so without bothering
to say anything. I think the best of
all prayers is just to kneel quietly
and let Jesus pour himself into
your soul.

WILLIAM DOYLE (1873–1917)

Once we see Jesus, the impossible
things he does in our lives become
as natural as breathing.

OSWALD CHAMBERS (1874–1917)

While he created the whole hierarchy
of the angels, the whole system of the
heavens, that activity could never alter
for a moment his eternal, inviolable
repose.

RONALD KNOX (1887–1957)

Prayer is essentially a love affair with
God.

MOTHER MARY CLARE (1906–88)

Prayer comes forth from my heart
as simply as a brook runs down to
a river. Prayer is simply love gushing
towards the beloved.

CATHERINE DE HUECK DOHERTY (1896–1985)

Forgiveness breaks the chain of
causality because he who forgives you
– out of love – takes upon himself the
consequences of what *you* have done.

DAG HAMMARSKJÖLD (1905–61)

When we truly love we are, by the
very nature of our love, compelled
to give. The more we pray, the more
we *want* to pray because God is
continually pouring the grace of prayer

and the longing for prayer into our hearts.

JOAN BARTLETT (1911–)

When God calls us he is not calling us primarily to do something, but to be something. Our calling, according to scripture, concerns much more our character and what kind of person we are than simply what our job is.

JOHN STOTT (1921–)

To follow Jesus is to walk step by step, not knowing what may be asked of you in the next quarter of an hour.

ROLAND WALLS (1917–)

This is our God, the Servant King, he calls us now to follow him, to bring our lives as a daily offering of worship to the Servant King.

GRAHAM KENDRICK (1950–)

25

Joy

In the Gospels, we are not told anything about Jesus' sense of humour – we do not know what made him laugh. Could he perhaps have had a gift for mimicry? When he told stories that involved direct quotation from an unidentified pillar of the religious establishment, could he have used the recognizable mannerisms and accent of a particular individual? If so, it would certainly have entertained his listeners – and would have done little to endear him to the ruling caste.

Sometimes it seems that humour and happiness have little to do with religion today. Some pillars of the religious

establishment still go about with long faces and appear to disapprove of the rest of us – an experience with which Jesus would have been very familiar. One of the principal objections lodged against him was that he would 'eat with tax collectors and sinners'. Happiness and joy are not an option, but an obligation for his followers, and in these selections from the writings of the mystics, we see that those who have truly 'fallen in love with God' overflow with God's own joy and delight.

Always be joyful; pray constantly; and for all things give thanks; this is the will of God for you in Christ Jesus.

1 THESSALONIANS 5:16–18

And you, Jesus, are you not also a mother? Are you not the mother who, like a hen, gathers her chickens under her wings?

ST ANSELM OF CANTERBURY (c. 1033–1109)

Thou hast the true and
    perfect gentleness,
no harshness hast thou
    and no bitterness:
O grant to us the grace
    we find in thee
that we may dwell in perfect unity.

JOHN CALVIN (1509–64)

Love and faithfulness always breed
confidence.

ST FRANCIS DE SALES (1567–1622)

I got me flowers to strew thy way;
I got me boughs off many a tree:
but thou wast up by break of day,
and brought'st thy sweets
    along with thee.

GEORGE HERBERT (1593–1633)

When sinks the soul, subdued by toil,
    to slumber,
  its closing eyes look up to you
    in prayer;
sweet the repose, beneath your wings
    o'ershadowing,

but sweeter still to wake
and find you there.

HARRIET BEECHER STOWE (1811–96)

Only in proportion as our own will is
surrendered are we able to discern
the splendour of God's will.

FRANCES HAVERGAL (1836–79)

O joy that seekest me through pain,
I cannot close my heart to thee;
I trace the rainbow through the rain,
and feel the promise is not vain,
that morn shall tearless be.

GEORGE MATHESON (1842–1906)

We live in an age of inventions. We
need no longer climb laboriously up
flights of stairs; in well-to-do houses
there are lifts. And I was determined
to find a lift to carry me to Jesus, for
I was far too small to climb the steep
stairs of perfection… It is your arms,
Jesus, that are the lift to carry me to
heaven.

ST THÉRÈSE OF LISIEUX (1873–97)

A smile costs nothing, but creates
much. It happens in a flash, but
the memory of it lasts for ever.
It cannot be begged, borrowed
or stolen, but it is of no earthly
use, or good, until it is given
away.

G.K. CHESTERTON (1874–1936)

The outpouring of his Holy Spirit
is really the outpouring of his love,
surrounding and penetrating your
little soul with a peaceful, joyful
delight in his creature: tolerant,
peaceful love full of longsuffering
and gentleness, working quietly,
able to wait for results, faithful,
devoted, without variableness
or shadow of turning. Such is the
charity of God.

EVELYN UNDERHILL (1875–1941)

O God, make all
the bad people good
and all the good people nice.

SOURCE UNKNOWN

Teach us to love and be loved in
perfect transparency.

DOM HÉLDER CÂMARA (1909–99)

Perfect joy lies in the utter
simplicity of peaceful love.
In order to shine out, such
joy requires no less than
your whole being.

ROGER SCHUTZ (1915–)

Fatherly and motherly love… since
the beginning of the world have been
pervaded by the mark and reflection
of the divine.

POPE JOHN PAUL II (1920–)

Every word that you find in
the Gospel is directed to you
personally, and if by flight of fancy
or imagination you were the only
person who ever existed, then
the Lord would have become
man, and the Gospel would have
been written, just for you.

CARDINAL BASIL HUME (1923–99)

Sing and dance together
    and be joyous,
  but let each of you be alone,
even as the strings of a lute are alone,
    though they quiver with
        the same music.

KAHLIL GIBRAN (1883–1931)

Alone and together we grope
forward like a driver in a fog seeing
only one or two Cat's-eyes ahead,
and having the option of stopping
still in fear or feeling ahead to the
emergence of the next Cat's-eye in
faith that it will be there… that he
will be there.

MICHAEL HOLLINGS (1921–97)

I am convinced that the modern way
to become holy is to do the will of
God. We do not have to enter a
convent or necessarily consecrate
ourselves to God or become priests.
No, it is enough to do what God
wants us to do.

CHIARA LUBICH (1920–)

Celebration is the sign that beyond all the sufferings, purifications and deaths, there is the eternal wedding feast, the great celebration of life with God. It is the sign that there is a personal meeting which will fulfil us, that our thirst for the infinite will be slaked and that the wound of our loneliness will be healed.

JEAN VANIER (1928–)

Jesus will finally and completely save his people, all people, from their sins… In a relationship with him that will never end, we will have what our hearts really desire and we will know that it is utterly worthwhile.

GERALD O'COLLINS (1931–)

Suffering

If there is a God, and he is all-good and all-powerful, how can he allow so much suffering in the world? None of the 'official' answers seems to deal adequately with the problem and mystery of suffering. Jesus, whom Christians believe to be the Son of God, suffered an appalling death by crucifixion. Why should an all-loving and all-powerful God allow his own Son to suffer? Many of the mystics were equally bewildered and angered by the problem of suffering. They cannot necessarily provide us with answers to the 'why' of evil and suffering, but they can perhaps help us to live with these realities, and to accept that, in some mysterious way, God has chosen to be alongside us in our pain and bewilderment.

The souls of the righteous are in the hand of God, and no torment will ever touch them. In the eyes of the foolish they seemed to have died, and their departure was thought to be a disaster, and their going from us to be their destruction; but they are at peace.

WISDOM 3:1–3

If we… offer ourselves to be shorn with that silent humility and patience in which he offered himself for us, he will take on himself the burdens of our fleeces, and will not disdain to carry the wool of his sheep. For he condescends to bring back to the fold on his shoulders the sheep which he has called back from sin.

ST PAULINUS OF NOLA (353/5–431)

He willed to suffer the sharpest pangs and deepest pains that ever were or ever shall be… yet even all this could not assuage his marvellous love. And he showed this in those high, wonderful words of love: 'If I could have suffered more, I would have suffered more.'

JULIAN OF NORWICH (c. 1342–AFTER 1416)

The devil sends me so offensive a spirit of bad temper that at times I think I could eat people up.

ST TERESA OF AVILA (1515–82)

Sorrow or trial lovingly submitted to does not prevent our being happy – it rather purifies the happiness.

BLESSED MARY MACKILLOP (1842–1909)

I believe that the divine heart is saddened much more by the thousand little acts of cowardice, and the carelessness of his friends, than by faults, even grave ones, that spring from our nature.

MAURICE BELLIÈRE (1874–1907)

I know that when the stress
    has grown too strong
  thou wilt be there.

I know that when the waiting
    seems so long
  thou hearest prayer.
I know that through the crash
    of falling worlds
  thou holdest me.
I know that life and death
    and all are thine
  eternally.

JANET ERSKINE STUART (1857–1914)

So long as there are poor,
  I am poor;
so long as there are prisons,
  I am a prisoner;
so long as there are sick,
  I am weak;
so long as there is ignorance,
  I must learn the truth;
so long as there is hate,
  I must love;
so long as there is hunger,
  I am famished.

Such is the identification our divine
Lord would have us make with all

whom he made in love and for love. Where we do not find love, we must put it. Then everyone is lovable.

FULTON SHEEN (1895–1979)

What we avert our eyes from one day is easily borne the next when we have learned a little more about love. Nurses know this, and so do mothers.

DOROTHY DAY (1897–1980)

I give advice that is rather more human and sympathetic than orthodox, and I not only temper the wind to the shorn lamb, but also to the neurotic sheep, whose need seems greater… I am so profoundly and always conscious of being a sinner myself, not in imagination but in reality and with a ghastly accumulation of irrefutable proof.

CARYLL HOUSELANDER (1901–54)

With him is all the strength of love and all the strength that turns the disillusion of love into that love which is stronger than death, into that unique love of Christ that can feed on its own fire and stay alive.

KARL RAHNER (1904–84)

Can God really suffer the loss of even the least of the sheep in his fold? One of his own creation, one for whom the Lord has shed his blood and endured the agony of being abandoned by the Father?

HANS URS VON BALTHASAR (1905–88)

Should it be ours to drain
    the cup of grieving
even to the dregs of pain,
    at thy command,
we will not falter, thankfully receiving
all that is given by thy loving hand.

DIETRICH BONHOEFFER (1906–45)

If I have the joy of possessing heaven,
I would not mind being in that heaven
near to those who today
declare themselves my enemies,
because there we will not be enemies.

OSCAR ROMERO (1917–80)

The cross tells us that God understands our sin and our suffering, for he took upon himself in the person of Jesus Christ our sins and our suffering. And from the cross, God declares, 'I love you. I know the heartaches and the sorrows and the pains that you feel. But I love you.'

BILLY GRAHAM (1918–)

Flinging oneself into the arms of the cross does not mean finding only suffering there. No, the cross leads to love, to the love which is the life of God himself within us.

CHIARA LUBICH (1920–)

A great purification will take place through the struggles of married life… This suffering can constitute a dark night that is no less purifying than St John of the Cross's dark night of the soul. And it leads to an intimacy and a union and a spiritual marriage that is consummated beyond the grave.

WILLIAM JOHNSTON (1925–)

Jesus did not promise to take away our burdens. He promised to help us carry them. And if we let go of ourselves – and our own resources – and allow the Lord to help us, we will be able to see death not as an enemy or a threat but as a friend.

CARDINAL JOSEPH BERNARDIN (1928–96)

My heart is little, fearful and very timid. It will always be so. But you say, 'Come to my heart. My heart is gentle and humble and very broken like yours. Do not be afraid. Come and let your heart find rest in mine and trust that all will be well.'

HENRI J.M. NOUWEN (1932–96)

You can shed tears that she is gone,
   or you can smile because
      she has lived.
You can close your eyes
      and pray that she'll come back,
   or you can open your eyes
      and see all she's left.

Your heart can be empty because
    you can't see her,
  or you can be full of the love
    you shared.
You can turn your back on tomorrow
    and live yesterday,
  or you can be happy for tomorrow
    because of yesterday.
You can remember her and only
    that she has gone,
  or you can cherish her memory
    and let it live on.
You can cry and close your mind,
    be empty and turn your back,
  or you can do what she'd want:
    open your eyes, love and go on.

FROM THE QUEEN MOTHER'S FUNERAL SERVICE

Living with Others

If you are one of those people who enjoys living alone, it is easy to start thinking that you are easy to get on with, because there is nobody around to ruffle your feathers! Nobody to bang on the bathroom door to make you hurry up in the morning; nobody to finish off the remains of the bottle of wine you had left in the fridge to go with your supper! However, a few days of joining in with family life is usually enough to convince us that we are still a little way short of sainthood! Living with other people is never easy, however fond we may be of our loved ones. Perhaps they insist on watching football on television when we want to see the soap operas (or vice versa), or they leave their dirty mugs and plates around the house instead of washing them up. It sometimes takes a little while for us to appreciate that we ourselves provide just as many sources of irritation for those who live with us. The mystics were only too aware of the daily annoyances as well as the joys of life with other people. These extracts from their writings emphasize the need for tolerance and acceptance – and also the joy of living closely united with God.

This is my commandment, that you love one another as I have loved you. No one has greater love than this, to lay down one's life for one's friends.

JOHN 15:12–13

When you set out to appear before the Lord, let the garment of your soul be woven throughout with the thread of wrongs no longer remembered.

ST JOHN CLIMACUS (c. 570–c. 649)

What happiness, what security, what joy to have someone to whom you dare to speak on terms of equality as to another self; one to whom you need have no fear to confess your failings; one to whom you can unblushingly make known what progress you have made in the spiritual life; one to whom you can entrust all the secrets of your heart and before whom you can place all your plans!

ST AELRED OF RIEVAULX (1109–67)

Preach the gospel, and sometimes use words.

ATTRIBUTED TO ST FRANCIS OF ASSISI

(c. 1181–1226)

Our Lord showed me an inward sight of his homely loving. I saw that he is everything that is good and comforting to us. He is our clothing. In his love he wraps and holds us. He enfolds us in love and he will never let us go.

JULIAN OF NORWICH (c. 1342–AFTER 1416)

Give me, Lord, a longing to be with you, not for the sake of avoiding the troubles of this world, nor for the sake of the joys of heaven, but simply for love of you.

ST THOMAS MORE (1478–1535)

Remember that there must be someone to cook the meals, and count yourselves happy in being able to serve like Martha.

ST TERESA OF AVILA (1515–82)

Whatever falls to thee to do, that perform as much as thou canst faithfully and diligently; but be not too anxious as to how it may turn out, nor whether it will be hazardous or not, but commit it to the good God.

MARY WARD (1585–1645)

Dear Jesus, we have little understanding and we are not able to see beyond our noses: if we were, we would be able to see the reason for what God does and we would have to praise and bless him, because that is the right thing in every way.

BLESSED DANIEL COMBONI (1831–81)

The more wit one has – and my friend, you have plenty of it – the more one must remember not to use this weapon too freely, for the sharpest swords make the most dangerous wounds.

MARIE ADELE GARNIER (1838–1924)

The more the soul forgets herself and gives herself up to the embrace of the love of Jesus, the more she enters into that peace of which it is said, 'Blessed are the peacemakers.'

CHARLES DE FOUCAULD (1858–1916)

Love one another, my dear children.
Seek rather what unites,
not what may separate you
   from one another.

POPE JOHN XXIII (1881–1963)

God, you have bound us together
in this bundle of life; give us grace
to understand how our lives depend
upon the courage, the industry, the
honesty and the integrity of others.

REINHOLD NIEBUHR (1892–1971)

We cannot love God unless we
love each other, and to love we must
know each other. We know him in the
breaking of bread, and we know each
other in the breaking of bread, and we
are not alone any more. Heaven is a
banquet and life is a banquet, too,
even with a crust, where there is
companionship.

We have all known the long
loneliness and we have learned that
the only solution is love and that love
comes with community.

DOROTHY DAY (1897–1980)

It is very often the little and the poor
who will evangelize you and reveal
Jesus to you.

LITTLE SISTER MAGDELEINE (1898–1989)

The Lamb passed into paradise;
   loud sang the cherubim.
For he came not alone
      to his Father's throne:
   Adam returned with him.

RACHEL HEATH (1897–1983)

I went through the city, realizing for the
first time in my life how good are all the
people in the world, and how much
value they have in the sight of God.

THOMAS MERTON (1915–68)

It may be necessary to defy despotic
governments, to stand by the

downtrodden and the underprivileged in the face of oppression and injustice. But 'perfect love casts out fear', and everything becomes possible when charitable projects are carried out with true charity in the heart.

AUNG SAN SUU KYI (1945–)

Never reproach somebody without first having let them know that you appreciate and love them. If they have the impression that you reject them and think them worthless, it makes it much harder for them to take criticism.

JEAN VANIER (1928–)

We are surrounded and enfolded with the loving care of divine providence; we have all we need to enter immediately upon a life of the greatest intimacy with God.

SOURCE UNTRACED

Growing Older

As we get older, it is easy to feel that we have never really done anything worthwhile. Perhaps life has been a mess and we leave behind us a trail of heartbreak and broken relationships, without any lasting achievement to show for it all. We had so many plans when we started out, and it has all turned to dust. The mystics were very familiar with the sense of desolation that descends when life does not come up to our expectations. It is easy to be very hard on ourselves and say, 'It is all my fault'; easy to believe that because we never wanted to have anything to do with God when things were going comparatively well, it is somehow unfair and 'too late' to start turning to him when the world is crashing

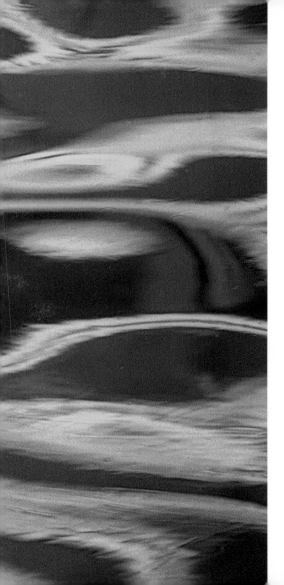

down around our ears. The message of the mystics is one of reassurance and unconditional love. It is precisely when it all seems too late and as if nobody really wants us that God longs to overwhelm us with his love.

I will pour out my spirit on all flesh;
your sons and your daughters
    shall prophesy,
    your old men shall dream dreams,
    and your young men shall see visions.

JOEL 2:28

Happy, indeed, is she to whom it is given to share this sacred banquet, to cling with all her heart to him.

ST CLARE (1193/4–1253)

Do not disdain your body.
For the soul is just as safe in its body
as in the kingdom of heaven.

ST MECHTILD OF MAGDEBURG (c. 1207–82)

Come, my joy, my love, my heart:
Such a joy, as none can move:

Such a love, as none can part:
Such a heart, as joys in love.

GEORGE HERBERT (1593–1633)

Just as I am, without one plea
but that thy blood was shed for me,
and that thou bidd'st me come to thee,
    O Lamb of God, I come.

Just as I am (thy love unknown
has broken every barrier down),
now to be thine, yea thine alone,
    O Lamb of God, I come.

CHARLOTTE ELLIOTT (1789–1871)

At this end of life, which seems to me
so near eternity, I am filled not only with
happiness in all the good God is giving
me, but in all that he has given me.

MOTHER MARIE ADELE GARNIER (1838–1924)

Thou art the way.
Hadst thou been nothing but the goal,
    I cannot say
if thou hadst ever met my soul.

ALICE MEYNELL (1847–1922)

I feel how powerless I am and I ask you
to 'clothe me with yourself', to identify
my soul with all the movements of your
soul, to immerse me in yourself, to take
possession of me, to substitute yourself
for me so that my life may be but a
radiance of your life.

BLESSED ELIZABETH OF THE TRINITY (1880–1906)

I've seen many people die in many diff-
erent ways, but I never get used to dying
and death. I always feel when I meet it
as if it comes for the first time, and I
uncover all my heart and mind humbly
before such uncomprehended royalty.

LAURENS VAN DER POST (1906–96)

Nothing is more practical
    than finding God.
That is, than falling in love
    in a quite absolute, final way.
What you are in love with,
    what seizes your imagination,
        will affect everything.
It will decide what will get you
    out of bed in the morning,

what you will do with your evenings,
   how you will spend your weekends,
what you read, whom you know,
   what breaks your heart,
what amazes you with joy and gratitude.
Fall in love, stay in love,
   and it will decide everything.

PEDRO ARRUPE (1907–91)

Jesus has so much to say about
listening and seeing, having our ears
and eyes open to others and for
others… So few people have time to
listen, to really listen. This takes time
and time is one of the commodities
we are given when we are old.

ELIZABETH BASSET (1908–2000)

Old age, well received, is a wonderful
opportunity for repairing lost chances.
As we grow older and feel the weight
of years, let us put ourselves totally into
the hands of the divine vine dresser that
he may accomplish in us all that we
promised to give him in our youth.

RUTH BURROWS (1923–)

Your longing for God is so deep, and yet he keeps himself away from you. He must be forcing himself to do so, because he loves you so much as to give Jesus to die for you and for me. Christ is longing to be your food… I know what you feel – terrible longing, with dark emptiness – and yet, he is the one in love with you.

MOTHER TERESA OF CALCUTTA (1910–97)

They raised you up on a cross. You took advantage of that to hold out your arms and draw people up to you. And countless people have come to the foot of the cross, to fling themselves into your arms.

POPE JOHN PAUL I (1912–78)

My infidelity to Christ, instead of making me sick with despair, drives me to throw myself all the more blindly into the arms of his mercy.

THOMAS MERTON (1915–68)

If we are to say that religion cannot be concerned with politics, then we are really saying that there is a substantial part of human life in which God's writ does not run. If it is not God's, then whose is it? Who is in charge if not the God and Father of our Lord Jesus Christ?

DESMOND TUTU (1931–)

Mighty Lord, in thy ascension we by faith behold our own.

CHRISTOPHER WORDSWORTH (1807–85)

We do not have to be saviours of the world! We are simply human beings, enfolded in weakness and in hope, called together to change our world one heart at a time.

JEAN VANIER (1928–)

I surrender to thee, O Most High,
    my poverty, my want and
        my weakness,
and thou givest me thy wealth.

SOURCE UNTRACED

Inner Peace

It is sometimes said that half the people in the world have too little time; we don't know where the day goes as we rush to get everything done. And the other half have too much time: the sick, the elderly and those in long-term care for whom the hours hang heavy. We all need to discover an inner 'core' of stillness and it isn't easy. The message of the mystics is that it is possible to find that inner peace, however difficult the outward circumstances. It takes time and concentration to carve out moments in the day for 'being' rather than 'doing', even if at first it feels like a waste of time. I have a friend who locks himself in the bathroom to meditate – seldom for more than three minutes at a time,

because a demanding job and a demanding family won't allow for more. Jesus understood the importance of 'wasting time with God', of getting away from those who desperately needed him, so that he could return to them with his batteries recharged.

Do not let your hearts be troubled. Believe in God, believe also in me. In my Father's house there are many dwelling places. If it were not so, would I have told you that I go to prepare a place for you? And if I go and prepare a place for you, I will come again and will take you to myself, so that where I am, there you may be also.

JOHN 14:1–3

Give us peace, Lord God, for you have given us all else; give us the peace that is repose, the peace of the sabbath, and the peace that knows no evening.

ST AUGUSTINE OF HIPPO (354–430)

Is the Spirit ever weary of loving? We find rest in those we love, and we provide a resting place in ourselves for those who love us.

ST BERNARD OF CLAIRVAUX (1090–1153)

How I long for you to set my whole being aflame with your presence, to consume me and transmute me, to make me one spirit with yourself.

ST THOMAS À KEMPIS (c. 1380–1471)

To God alone be the glory, for it is he that does all things.

BLESSED MARIE OF THE INCARNATION (1599–1672)

Tranquillity of soul consists
    in this alone,
to be united whole to God,
    a oned one.

ANGELUS SILESIUS (1624–77)

Acquire inward peace, and thousands around you will find their salvation.

ST SERAPHIM OF SAROV (1759–1833)

Shine from the cross to me,
    then all is peace;
shine from the throne,
    then all my troubles cease;
speak but the word,
    and sadness quits my soul;
touch but my hand with thine,
    and I am whole.

HORATIUS BONAR (1808–82)

I am so weak that I can hardly write, I cannot read my Bible, I cannot even pray, I can only lie still in God's arms like a little child, and trust.

HUDSON TAYLOR (1832–1905)

If only we could be content to look with trustful, uncritical gaze on everything which it is not our direct duty to attend to, knowing that God is over all, that he is wiser and more powerful than we can understand, and that he can be trusted with the management of his own creation.

DANIEL CONSIDINE (1849–1922)

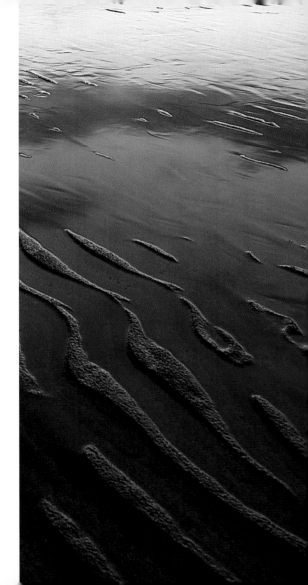

If I see Jesus patiently waiting for me to come back to him, and giving me a new grace after I have asked him to forgive me for committing yet another fault, I am conquered and climb right back into the saddle. What sometimes holds me back now is not Jesus but my own self. I am ashamed of myself, and instead of throwing myself into the arms of this friend, I scarcely drag myself to his feet.

MAURICE BELLIÈRE (1874–1907)

Let us rejoice in the great adoring acts and splendid heroisms of God's great lovers, and humbly do the little we can. We too have our place.

EVELYN UNDERHILL (1875–1941)

We have been looking at the ground so long that we have forgotten that the stars still shine.

GEORGES VANIER (1888–1967)

Forgiveness is the key that unlocks the door of resentment and the handcuffs

of hate. It is a power that breaks the chains of bitterness and the shackles of selfishness. He who cannot forgive others breaks the bridge over which he himself must pass.

CORRIE TEN BOOM (1892–1983)

If we fall in love with the crucified one, we shall know joy beyond all knowing. We shall have peace, the peace he promised.

CATHERINE DE HUECK DOHERTY (1896–1985)

Love is going out of oneself, surrendering the self, letting the reality, the truth, take over… It is not something we achieve for ourselves. It is something that comes when we let go.

BEDE GRIFFITHS (1906–93)

Do with me as you will, Lord. I place no obstacles, I make no reservations. For you are my whole delight and the love of my soul, and to you, in turn, I pour out the confidences of my heart.

ST FAUSTINA KOWALSKA (1904–38)

I realize that the more I speak, the
more I will need silence to remain
faithful to what I say.

HENRI J.M. NOUWEN (1932–96)

We have lived off the outside of our
faith for too long – maybe what we
have got to learn is to return to the
depth of faith.

GEORGE CAREY (1935–)

Has it ever occurred to you that
Jesus, that master in the art of prayer,
would take the trouble to walk up
a hill in order to pray? Like all great
contemplatives he was aware that
the place in which we pray has an
influence on the quality of our prayer.

ANTHONY DE MELLO (1931–87)

I am a wounded child,
  resting,
peaceful in the folds
  of a Father's arms;
    asleep.

MAUREEN McCARTHY (1936–99)

May God, who loved you into being
  to share his life,
now nourish you and make you strong,
and shed his light upon your path;
may he walk the road with you
  and lead you home.

PAUL BROWNE (1951–)

Text Acknowledgments

pp. 12, 36, 43, 51, 57: the scripture quotations contained herein are from the New Revised Standard Version of the Bible, Anglicized Edition, copyright © 1989, 1995 by the Division of Christian Education of the National Council of the Churches of Christ in the United States of America, and are used by permission. All rights reserved.

p. 16: extract from 'Love: A Prayer' by Diana Momber, from *Towards the Light*, published by Pentland Books, 2001. Copyright © 2001 Diana Momber.

p. 20: extract from the Revised English Bible with the Apocrypha copyright © 1989 by Oxford University Press and Cambridge University Press.

p. 21: extract by St John of the Cross, from *Centred on Love: The Poems of St John of the Cross*, translated by Marjorie Flower OCD, published by The Carmelite Nuns, Varroville, NSW Australia, 1983.

p. 25: extract from 'From heaven you came' ('The Servant King') by Graham Kendrick, copyright © 1983 Thankyou Music. Administered by worshiptogether.com songs, excluing UK and Europe, administered by Kingsway Music. tym@kingsway.co.uk. Used by permission.

p. 27: extract taken from the New Jerusalem Bible, published & copyright © 1985 by Darton, Longman & Todd Ltd & les Editions du Cerf, & by Doubleday, a division of Bantam Doubleday Dell Publishing Group, Inc. Used by permission of Darton, Longman & Todd Ltd, & Doubleday, a division of Random House, Inc.

p. 37: extract from 'Powers of Good' by Dietrich Bonhoeffer, from *Letters and Papers from Prison*, The Enlarged Edition, SCM Press, 1971.

p. 47: extract from 'Love Triumphant' by Rachel Heath.

p. 61: extract from 'Millennium' by Maureen McCarthy, from *Prelude to Passion: Journey of Love*, published by St Bede's Publications, Massachussetts. Copyright © 1999 Maureen McCarthy.

p. 61: 'Viaticum' is taken from *Letting Go* by Paul Browne OSB, published by Ampleforth Abbey, York, YO62 4EN. Copyright © 2001 Paul Browne and Ampleforth Abbey Trustees.